First World War
and Army of Occupation
War Diary
France, Belgium and Germany

40 DIVISION
Divisional Troops
Divisional Trench Mortar Batteries
6 June 1916 - 27 April 1918

WO95/2599/3

The Naval & Military Press Ltd
www.nmarchive.com
Published in association with The National Archives

Published by

The Naval & Military Press Ltd

Unit 10 Ridgewood Industrial Park,

Uckfield, East Sussex,

TN22 5QE England

Tel: +44 (0) 1825 749494

www.naval-military-press.com

www.nmarchive.com

This diary has been reprinted in facsimile from the original. Any imperfections are inevitably reproduced and the quality may fall short of modern type and cartographic standards.

© Crown Copyright
Images reproduced by permission of The National Archives, London, England, 2015.

Contents

Document type	Place/Title	Date From	Date To
Heading	WO95/2599/3		
Heading	40th Division 40th Divl Ammn Column Jun 1916-Mar 1919		
Heading	War Diary of 40th DAC RFA		
War Diary	Harve	06/06/1916	09/06/1916
War Diary	Nedonchelle	09/06/1916	09/06/1916
War Diary	Verquin	10/06/1916	03/07/1916
War Diary	Houchin	04/07/1916	04/12/1916
War Diary	Labeuvriere	06/12/1917	06/12/1917
War Diary	La Thieuloye	07/12/1916	07/12/1916
War Diary	Concay Sur Canche	08/12/1916	08/12/1916
War Diary	Authieule	09/12/1916	09/12/1916
War Diary	Talmas	10/12/1916	12/12/1916
War Diary	Allery	10/12/1916	29/12/1916
War Diary	St Sauveur	30/12/1916	30/12/1916
War Diary	Vaux	31/12/1916	31/12/1916
War Diary	Bray	31/12/1916	09/03/1917
War Diary	P.C. 6 L 18 ao7	15/03/1917	21/04/1917
War Diary	Moislains	21/04/1917	26/04/1917
War Diary	Manancourt	28/04/1917	08/07/1917
War Diary	Nurlu	12/07/1917	27/10/1917
War Diary	Perunne	31/10/1917	31/10/1917
War Diary	Trescault	01/12/1917	03/12/1917
War Diary	K 17d	05/12/1917	05/12/1917
War Diary	Bertincourt	09/12/1917	12/12/1917
War Diary	Hamelincourt	12/12/1917	22/03/1918
War Diary	Berles au Bois	14/05/1918	14/05/1918
War Diary	Saulty	30/05/1918	31/05/1918
War Diary	Gaudiempre	23/06/1918	23/06/1918
War Diary	Gaudiempre	20/06/1918	20/06/1918
War Diary	Barly	24/06/1918	26/06/1918
War Diary	Fosseux	26/07/1918	01/08/1918
War Diary	Gouy	01/08/1918	27/08/1918
War Diary	Gouy	25/08/1918	25/08/1918
War Diary	Metcatel	01/09/1918	24/10/1918
War Diary	Lannoy	08/11/1918	15/11/1918
War Diary	Lannoy	11/11/1918	11/11/1918
War Diary	Wambrechies	11/11/1918	31/03/1919
Heading	40th Divisional Artillery. 40th Divisional Ammunition Column R.F.A. April 1918		
War Diary	Simencourt	06/04/1918	27/04/1918

W005/2599/3

40TH DIVISION

40TH DIVL AMMN COLUMN
JUN 1916-MAR 1919

40 JUMS
40 DAC

Vol 1

WAR DIARY
or
INTELLIGENCE SUMMARY

War diary of 40th Div. R.A.

Army Form C. 2118.

WAR DIARY or INTELLIGENCE SUMMARY.

(Erase heading not required.)

June

Instructions regarding War Diaries and Intelligence Summaries are contained in F. S. Regs., Part II. and the Staff Manual respectively. Title pages will be prepared in manuscript.

Place	Date	Hour	Summary of Events and Information	Remarks and references to Appendices
HARVE	6-6-16	12 o/c	4th arrived at LE HAVRE in two trainloads. NIRVANA + BELLEROPHON. The unit was accommodated in Camp 2 SANVIC. Strength + establishment arrived as under:	
			O/r O.R. Horses Mules 13 s wagon 4 s wagon G.S. wagon GS limber	
			Strength 16 318 510 528 13 47 16 0 15	
			Estab. 16 318 510 548 16 48 16 78 15	
	7-6-16		The unit commenced entrainings for the concentration area on the morning of 7th June in trainloads of 2 offrs 115 O.R. 160 animals 27 vehicles. Three trains were despatched on the 7th with the bulk of 1, 2 + 3 sections respectively. No 4 Section + details "a echelon proceeded to Ordnance Depot HARVE to draw harness for 78 6 horse teams + 78 G.S. wagons. As soon as the issue was completed animals were harnessed up + hooked in + it proceeded to Shed R to load up the ammunition + stores. Wagons were parked for the night on the Quinner Quay + horses + men in HALLE 3 + Camp 5 respectively.	
	8-6-16		The remainder of the column left HARVE in 4 trains	

Army Form C. 2118.

WAR DIARY
or
INTELLIGENCE SUMMARY.
(Erase heading not required.)

Place	Date	Hour	Summary of Events and Information	Remarks and references to Appendices
HARVE	8-6-16		Headquarters travelling with last 2 which left at 20.59 arriving	
	9-6-16		at LILLERS at 17.0 on the 9th June	
			The Column was accommodated in billets around NEDONCHELLE	
NEDONCHELLE			6 miles S.W. of LILLERS. Orders were issued directing that the	
			Section be attached to divisions of 1st Corps for instruction as follows :-	
			No 1 Section to 16th Division at VERQUIN	
			No 3 " " 15th " at VERQUINEUL	
			No 2 " " 1st " at HOUCHIN	
			H.Q. " " 16th " at VERQUIN	
			B Echelon " " 1st + 16th " s at HESDINGNEUIL	
VERQUIN	10/6/16	9.0.	A Echelon + Headquarters marched to their respective Division	
			as above in very heavy rain.	
	11/6/16	9.0.	B Echelon marched to HESDINGNEUL	Ref FRANCE 1/40,000 Sheet 36b
			Section report centres were located as follows	
			H.Q. E 29 q 7.7 No 2 Hq q.0 B Echelon E 25 5.5.	
			No 1 E 28 b 9.9 No 3 F 25 c 4.3	

Army Form C. 2118.

WAR DIARY
or
INTELLIGENCE SUMMARY.
(Erase heading not required.)

Place	Date	Hour	Summary of Events and Information	Remarks and references to Appendices
VERQUIN	11-6-16		Section were split up amongst the Batteries they were attached to for instruction	
	16-6-16		Section were refused as complete section & received attached to their respective divisions. They were not administered by the O.C. 40th Bac. but acted entirely under the orders of the O.C. Div. to which they were attached. No ammunition returns were kept & Batteries of 1st Corps division were supplied with ammunition as well as 40th Divnl Batteries.	
	29-6-16		No 4427 Dr Powles S.W. No 4 Section was wounded. Two men killed & 2 wounded at LOOS	
	26-6-16		Orders were received for the return of 255 rifles thus reducing the number carried from 615 to 260	
Rillette	2-7-16		With the exception of No 1 Section under canvas all Section were	

R.R. Smith
Lt.-Colonel, R.F.A.
COMDG. 40TH DIV. AMN. COL. B.E.F.

Army Form C.2118.

WAR DIARY
or
INTELLIGENCE SUMMARY.
(Erase heading not required.)

Ref 1/40,000 FRANCE sheet 36B

Vol

4th July
D.A.C.

Place	Date	Hour	Summary of Events and Information	Remarks and references to Appendices
VERQUIN	3/7/16	16.00	Received orders for 40th D.A.C. to relieve 1st D.A.C. "A" Echelon at HOUCHIN "B" Echelon as HESDINGNEUIL on 4th July	
HOUCHIN	4/7/16		Move completed. Head Quarters established at K.16.a.1.8. Bty wagon lines located as follows	
			178 181 187	
			A L.19.c.7.5 A L.19.c.4.5 A L.25.c.4.5 A L.19.c.5.1	
			B K.29.d.9.9 B L.25.a.9.0 B L.31.a.6.8 B L.25.a.6.7	
			C L.19.a.2.2 C K.24.b.8.6 C L.31.a.3.9 C L.19.c.6.3	
			D L.19.c.4.8 D K.25.c.7.0 D L.25.a.8.7 D L.31.a.6.3	
HOUCHIN	5/7/16		D/181 changed wagon line to L.33.b.4.9.	
HOUCHIN	6/7/16		In accordance with orders from 40th Divn. 13 limbered wagons were exchanged for 13 S.A.A. carts, 1 from each Battalion of infantry in 40th Divn. On the 25th the 2 remaining limbered wagons were exchanged for SAA carts with 8th Division	

Army Form C. 2118.

WAR DIARY
or
INTELLIGENCE SUMMARY.
(Erase heading not required.)

Place	Date	Hour	Summary of Events and Information	Remarks and references to Appendices
HOUCHIM	9/7/16		D/155 Bde. 32nd Division attached to 40th D.A.C. for ammunition supply. Wagon line located at L.13.c.6.6.	
			During the month of July ammunition was supplied to Btys as under:—	
			175th A 1573 151st A 1141 155th A 1522 185th A 1522	
			B 1357 B 1825 B 1363 B 1266	
			C 797 C 955 C 620 C 1253	
			D 1529 D 63 D 541 D 454	
			Total 5284 4020 3340 4885	
			Grand Total 17,529 rounds	
			The longest amount of ammunition issued to any unit at one time was 605 rds issued to A/155 on July 15th.	
			796,000 rounds S.A.A. were issued to 40th Division Infantry during the month.	

Army Form C. 2118.

WAR DIARY
or
INTELLIGENCE SUMMARY.
(Erase heading not required.)

Instructions regarding War Diaries and Intelligence Summaries are contained in F. S. Regs., Part II. and the Staff Manual respectively. Title pages will be prepared in manuscript.

(3)

Place	Date	Hour	Summary of Events and Information	Remarks and references to Appendices
In the Field			There were no casualties during the month of July. One man 14195 Dr W. Welding was killed by falling from a mule on 11-7-16. Seven men were evacuated through accident + sickness	

A D Smith
Lt.-COLONEL, R.F.A.
COMDG. 40TH DIV. AMN. COL. R.F.A.

40th Bde R.F.A.

WAR DIARY
or
INTELLIGENCE SUMMARY.
(Erase heading not required.)

Army Form C.2118.
40th BDE. R.MN. COL.
No. 116/72
Date 1/9/16

August, 1916

Place	Date	Hour	Summary of Events and Information	Remarks and references to Appendices
HOURGE	4/8/16		D/155th Bde R.F.A, 32nd Divn ceased to be officiated to the Bde. for ant: supply	
	11/8/16		On the night 11/12th August the 40th Divnl Arty was re-grouped owing to change in front occupied by 40th Divn. The Bde. were not affected.	
	25/8/16		On the night 25th & 26th August the Divnl Arty was again regrouped owing to an extension of the front held by 40th Divn & the following units were attached to the Bde. for anti-aircraft supply	
			to No 1 Section A/169th + D/169th Bde	
			" No 2 " 118th Infantry Brigade	
			" No 3 " C/306th Bde. C/307th	
	30/8/16		A further regrouping of the Divnl Arty took place in the night of the 30/31st without affecting the Bde.	
			Orders were received regarding re-organisation of Arty Brigades as follows 155th Bde to be reduced + absorbed by 17th + 131st Bde except D/155th which is to form C/188th & C/351st were the present C/188th	

Army Form C. 2118.

WAR DIARY
or
INTELLIGENCE SUMMARY. August (Sheet 2)
(Erase heading not required.)

Instructions regarding War Diaries and Intelligence Summaries are contained in F. S. Regs., Part II. and the Staff Manual respectively. Title pages will be prepared in manuscript.

Place	Date	Hour	Summary of Events and Information	Remarks and references to Appendices
HOUCHIN	30/8/16		which is to be absorbed by A + B Btys. The Divisional, well then consist of 3 city Bdes 2 with three 6 gun 18 pdr Btys + 1 four gun 4.5 how + one (the 153rd) with two 6 gun 18 pdrs and one four gun 4.5 how Bty. This change to take effect from 1st September. In anticipation of the above the following changes were made in the Bde on the 31st August. Btys were re-affiliated to sections as under No 1 Section 173rd Bde No 2 " 171st Bde. No 3 " 172nd Bde and in order to facilitate supply 18 pdr + 4.5 ammunition wagons were allotted to gun and section as per gun + howitzer in their affiliated Bde. Wagons per section are now as under No 1 Section 15 – 15 pdr 4 – 4.5 No 2 " 15 – 15 " 4 – 4.5 No 3 " 15 – 15 " 8 – 4.5.	

WAR DIARY or INTELLIGENCE SUMMARY

Army Form C. 2118.

August 16 (Sheet 3)

Place	Date	Hour	Summary of Events and Information	Remarks and references to Appendices
HOUCHIN	12.8.16		On the 12th of August a new system of ant. supply came into force whereby the Sub Park ceased to deliver ammunition &c. drawn direct from Railhead in their own transport. On the 31st August ammunition was supplied direct from Railway trucks at VERQUIGNEUL instead of from LAPUGNOY as heretofore. Ammunition was delivered to Batteries etc. during the month as follows:- A/76 2375 A 191 1929 A 188 2144 D 169-241 B 4091 B 1064 B 759 B 1266 C/306-305 C 4155 C 2826 C 1555 C 1544 D 634 D 500 D 1738 D 1291 —————— —————— —————— —————— 11,255 6319 3395 6245 546 Total 25,187 of which 2,544 were 4.5 inch. 11.9A How. Batt. 250,000 rds SAA 170,000 " SAA 332,600 " SAA ——————— Total 752,600	

WAR DIARY
or
INTELLIGENCE SUMMARY.

Army Form C. 2118.

August '16 Sheet 4

Place	Date	Hour	Summary of Events and Information	Remarks and references to Appendices
HOUCHIN	31-7-16		Trench mortar + grenade issues were as follows	

Stokes rifle grenades 10,705
Mills hand "   9,324
Newton pitcher   14,976
3" Stokes gun   9,562
Very light, doses,   430
9.45 T.M.   50
2" T.M.   2,440

Captain of Ward was attached to D/176 for one month on 16/8/16 for duty. A nursing sister attached to the B.G.E. from here dealt in exchange. 2nd/Lt. S.M. Glubtstein was evacuated to War Riding C.C.S. on 25/7/16. C 07/B
Capt. R. Cave-Brown-Cave admitted to 137th Fd Amb 31-8-16.
Reinforcements received during the month amounted to 23 other ranks and 14 men were evacuated.
On the 17th August orders were issued transferring all the personnel of Medium + Heavy Trench Mortar Batteries to the Bde Am

Army Form C. 2118.

WAR DIARY
or
~~INTELLIGENCE~~ SUMMARY.

(Erase heading not required.)

August 1916 (Sheet-5)

Place	Date	Hour	Summary of Events and Information	Remarks and references to Appendices
HOUCHIN			the establishment of a D.A.C. was increased by 15 gunners from this date.	
			With the exception of one horse killed by hostile shell fire in BETHUNE on the 7th August, no casualties due to enemy have occurred during August.	

Peter Wright
Lt-Colonel, R.F.A.
COMDG. 40TH DIV. AMN. COL. R.F.A.

WAR DIARY or INTELLIGENCE SUMMARY

Army Form C.2118.
F.A. W24

September 1916

Place	Date	Hour	Summary of Events and Information	Remarks and references to Appendices
HOUCHIN	1-9-16		On the re-organization of the Divnl. Arty in 3 mixed Brigades the wagon lines were situated as follows:— A178 L19 c.3.6 A181 L 19 c 4.5 A 158 h19 c 31 B " K24 d 9.9 B " L 31 a 6.5 B " h19 c 63 C " L19 c 4.5 C " K 24 b 6.6 C " L25 c 45 D " L19 c 4.7 D " L 33 b 6.9 D " L31 a 4.1	Ref Chart Sct NW 1/40000
	11-9-16		14th Div ammn column has been lent to the 3rd Divn + the sections attached for ammn supply A/169 D/169 C/306 ceased to be attached for ammn supply C/307	
	23-9-16		14th Div section was again taken over by 40th Divn + C/161 attached to no 3 section for ammn supply. Wagon line at E 19 d 9.9	
			During the month, the ammunition has been delivered by the D.A.S.P. G.A.S wagons have drawn ammn as required from	

Army Form C. 2118.

WAR DIARY
or
INTELLIGENCE SUMMARY.
(Erase heading not required.)

Sheet 2
September 1916

Place	Date	Hour	Summary of Events and Information	Remarks and references to Appendices
HOUCHIN.			LAPUGNOY (1st Corps Reullieux) VERQUIGNEUL HALTE (advanced railhead) and 1st Corps Reserve dump at K11 central	
			Ammunition has been issued as follows	
			A 178 1422 A 151 1666 A 185 1936 A 169 798	
			B " 1811 B " 1240 B " 2673 D 169 264	
			C " 657 C " 1855 C " 1404 C 306 382	
			D " 897 D " 1404 D " 1457 C 307 130	
			Total 4787 Total 6165 7470 1544	
			Grand total 19,966 of which 4992 were 4.5 hows.	
			Small arms amm. — grenades and S.A.A.	
			No 3 rifle 9100 No 23 rifle 900 3" Stokes 14,361	
			No 5 hand 12360 Very lights (1 vol) 161 2" T.M. 5613	
			Newton pipper 16308 9.45" T.M. 80 S.A.A. 14,720,000	

Army Form C. 2118.

Sheet 3
September 1916

WAR DIARY
or
INTELLIGENCE SUMMARY.
(Erase heading not required.)

Place	Date	Hour	Summary of Events and Information	Remarks and references to Appendices
HOUCHIN			The following changes took place amongst the officers during the month:- F.W. BRISCOE posted to No 3 Section from B/175 1-9-16. CAPT R. CAVE-BROWN-CAVE evacuated sick 5-9-16. Lt H. HARMAN transferred to 55th Divn 12-9-16. CAPT. G.D. WARD handed over command of No 3 Section on being posted to D/175 Bde. 2/Lt W. BAKER posted to B battery from 161st Bde. 12-9-16. SERGT MAJOR (W.O) was demonstrated under 4-9-16. Twenty-three men were evacuated through sickness + eighteen horses.	

A.D. Dunlop.
Lt-Colonel, R.F.A.
Comdg De 20TH Divl ...

Army Form C. 2118.

40 / October 1916 / D.A.E. Vol 5

WAR DIARY
or
INTELLIGENCE SUMMARY.
(Erase heading not required.)

Place	Date	Hour	Summary of Events and Information	Remarks and references to Appendices
HOUCHIN	3rd		C/161 and C/188 were temporarily withdrawn from 40th Divnl Arty and sent to XI Corps area.	40th D.A.O. no 7 d/3/10/16
	10th		The MAROC section was handed over to the 37th Divn IV Corps. The change did not in any way affect the 40th D.A.C.	40th D.A.O.5 d/8/10/16
	12th		The 40th Division took over from the 8th the HULLUCH sector and the 40th D.A. was grouped as follows. Right group (LOOS) A/175 B/175 351 A 351 B (army C) 351 D Centre group (14 BIS) A/175 (army 4) B/175 351 E 351 C Left group (HULLUCH) A/175 (2 guns) B/175 351 F 351 D (1 howr) No wagon lines were changed.	40th D.A.O. no 9 d/9/10/16

Army Form C. 2118.
(Sheet 2)

WAR DIARY
or
INTELLIGENCE SUMMARY.
(Erase heading not required.)

October 16

Place	Date	Hour	Summary of Events and Information	Remarks and references to Appendices
HOUCHIN	15th		C/165 returned to 40th D.A. and came under Lt. Grant.	
			Orders were received to prepare to move.	
	3 AM		24th Divn took over the line from 40th Divn. Our infantry were withdrawn and relieved by Infantry Bdes as under. 12th Inf Bde by 72nd on night 25/26th October 12th " 17th " 27/28th October 11th " 73rd " 29/30th October Infantry Bdes were attached to Sectors as follows:- 17th Infantry Bde – No 1 Section 72nd " No 2 " 73rd " No 3 " General Code letters for units were introduced during the month as follows 2" TM = TMB 3" TM = TMC	

WAR DIARY
or
INTELLIGENCE SUMMARY
(Erase heading not required.)

Army Form C. 2118.

October 1916
Sheet 3

Place	Date	Hour	Summary of Events and Information	Remarks and references to Appendices

HOUCHIN

9.45" T.M. T.M.F.

A new method of holding ammunition was instituted at the Corps on 27th October whereby out of a total of 354 rds. allot. for each 17 lm. gun 176 are unboxed and 178 boxed. The whole of the above to be held by the Battery at guns and wagon line, no ammn. being held by the D.A.C. at all.

Ammn. has been delivered during October as follows:-

```
A  175   930      A  151  1704     A  385  17021   C  191  246
B  "     1703     B   "   754      B   "   1818
C  "     1901     C   "   1678     C   "    415
D  "     1466     D   "   1020     D   "   1227
total    6060         5256               5168        246
```

Grand total 16,724 of which 4128 was 4.5 how.

Army Form C. 2118.

WAR DIARY
or
INTELLIGENCE SUMMARY.
(Erase heading not required.)

October 16
Sheet 4

Place	Date	Hour	Summary of Events and Information	Remarks and references to Appendices
HEUCHIN			Grand Totals of Grenades and S.A.A.	
			Hales No 5 Rifle 5600 3" TM 16,530 S.A.A. 1,562,000.	
			Mills No 5 Red 9620 2" TM 3250	
			Newton Pitcher 10,324 9.45" TM 60	
			No 23 Rifle 480 Very Lights 303 boxes	
			There were no casualties affecting officers during the	
			month of October.	
			37 Rank and file reinforcements reported for duty.	
			16 animals were evacuated.	

A.M.Dunlop
LT.-COLONEL, R.F.A.
COMDG. 40TH DIV. AMN. COL. B.E.F.

WAR DIARY or INTELLIGENCE SUMMARY.

Army Form C. 2118.

40D Army Cor[?]
NOVEMBER 1916
Vol 6

Place	Date	Hour	Summary of Events and Information	Remarks and references to Appendices
HOUCHIN	Nov 1st		The 40th D.A.C. continued to remain attached to 24th Div. during the month of November. And with the exception of a slight alteration of groups entailed by transfer of 1 Section A/175 from Left to Centre group + 1 Section A/178 from Right group to Left group there were no change in the disposition of the 4 D.A.C. groups. The above change did not affect the D.A.C. During the month fatigue parties were found nightly as under 1 NCO + 20 men assisting the Army Troops Engineer Coy in the erection of light railways. Two parties each of 1 NCO + 15 men to carry Trench Mortar Ammunition from Bomb Stores to T.M. emplacements. In addition D.A.C. teams have been used for replacing gas cylinders in the line.	
	30th		Orders were received for the transfer of the 40th D.A. from the 1st Corps 1st Army to the 1st Corps 4th Army. 40th D.A. to march from HOUCHIN to LABEURIÈRE	NQ90 10 d/- 30/11/16

2nd Sheet Army Form C. 2118.

NOVEMBER 16

WAR DIARY
or
INTELLIGENCE SUMMARY.

Place	Date	Hour	Summary of Events and Information	Remarks and references to Appendices
HOUCHIN	Nov 1		Preceded on relief by 24th D.L.I. Ammunition was issued during the month as follows:—	

```
A  171  1064        A 151   750     A 188   1206
B   "   1400        B 151  1957     B 188   1024
C   "   1350        C 151  3829     C 188    911
D   "   1075        D 151  2338     D 188    835
        4839              8874              3976
```

Grand total 17639 of which 5159 were 4.5 hour.
Trench mortar and grenades were issued as follows:
Flares No 3 Rifle 5900   3" TM 5703   SAA 1,490,000.
Mills nos Round   3560   2" TM 3920
Hunter Pattern   8734   945TM   30

2/Lieut Geo. F R Price was admitted to hospital 5/11/16
2 " S.m. Wycheloin was admitted to hospital 21/11/16
2/Lt. H.L. Webber was posted to No1 Station and joined for

Army Form C. 2118.

3rd Sheet
NOVEMBER '16.

WAR DIARY
or
INTELLIGENCE SUMMARY.
(Erase heading not required.)

Place	Date	Hour	Summary of Events and Information	Remarks and references to Appendices
HOUCHIN	Duty 30/11/16. 2/SF Whey Deacon was posted to No 3 Section 30/11/16. 10/104 Gunner H Wakeling No 1 Section died in 11th Hon at No 1 Casualty Clearing Station of Aluminium 50 Rank and file reinforcements were received during November.			

R. Mushm
LT.-COLONEL, R.F.A.
COMMDR. 40TH DIV. AMN. COL. R.F.A.

WAR DIARY
or
INTELLIGENCE SUMMARY

Army Form C. 2118.

DECEMBER 1916

Place	Date	Hour	Summary of Events and Information	Remarks and references to Appendices
HOUCHIN	Dec. 1916 4		The 40th T.M.C. having handed over to the 24th T.M.C. marched to LABEUVIERE en route for the XV Corps area. "A" Echelon filled up with ammunition less grenades from the 1st Reserve dump on the CHOQUES – LAPUGNOY road on the 5th. "B" Echelon remained empty.	Maps. Sheet 36B 1/40,000
LABEUVIERE	6th		The march was continued both echelons joining up at LA THIEULOYE	"
LA THIEULOYE	7th		HQ, No 3 Section + B Echelon moved to CONCHY-SUR-CANCHE No 1 + 2 Sections + A Echelon to AUBREMETZ	LENS 11 1/100,000
CONCHY SUR CANCHE	8th		The Column marched via DOULLENS to AUTHIEULE	"
AUTHIEULE	9th		The Column marched to TALMAS	"
TALMAS	11th		Orders were received for "A" Echelon to proceed to join the line to be affiliated to the 33rd Divn. Head Quarters + B Echelon	

WAR DIARY
or
INTELLIGENCE SUMMARY.
(Erase heading not required.)

Army Form C. 2118.

DECEMBER 1916 Sheet-2

Place	Date	Hour	Summary of Events and Information	Remarks and references to Appendices
TALMAS	10th		proceeding to ALLERY then to rest. The column split-up on 10th inter as follows. HQ Quarters & B Echelon marched via CANAPLES AMIENS VIGNACOURT-HANGEST-ARRAINE to ALLERY. No.1 Section to Camp 14, 3 miles W. of BRAY. No 2 & 3 Sections remained at TALMAS.	ALLERY 6 11 AMIENS 17 DIEPPE 16.
	11th		No 1 Section marched from Camp 14 to a position about ½ mile NE of BRAY & commenced supplying ammunition to the 178th Bde. No 2 Section marched to Camp 14. HQ & B Echelon came under the administration of 5th Divl Arty and commenced training in accordance with a programme approved of by B.G. R.A. 5th Divn.	
	12th		No 2 Section marched to a position adjacent to No 1 Section & commenced supply of ammunition to the 131st Bde. No 3 Section marched to Camp 14. As the XV Corps relieved the French Army on this front a great deal of very heavy work devolved on "A" Echelon in providing a dump of 6,000 rds per gun at the gun pits.	

WAR DIARY

Army Form C. 2118.

DECEMBER 1916.
Sheet 3

Place	Date	Hour	Summary of Events and Information	Remarks and references to Appendices
ALLERY	Dec 18th to 19th		Ammunition was drawn from PLATEAU siding S.W. of MARICOURT and conveyed as close to guns as possible in wagons the final stages being unbent by pack horse. The round journey from Q.C. to gun position via PLATEAU and returning being about 14 miles & the time occupied often reaching 15 hours owing to the congestion at railheads & the heavy nature of the ground. During the period 18th to 29th ammn was delivered to Batteries as follows. A.178 B.178 C.178 D.178 A.181 B.181 C.181 D.181 3144O 3684 3652 2304 4250 3296 3278 1485 Total 18 Dec 22,400 Total w.e. 3992 grand total 26592 ans. In addition large numbers of horses were lent to batteries to assist in packing amm across different country.	AMIENS 1/100,000
ALLERY	29th		H.Q. & B Echelon marched from ALLERY to ST SAUVEUR	

WAR DIARY or INTELLIGENCE SUMMARY.

Army Form C. 2118.

DECEMBER /16 Sheet 4

Place	Date	Hour	Summary of Events and Information	Remarks and references to Appendices
ST SAUVEUR	30th		The march was continued to VAUX-SUR-SOMME	
VAUX	31st		No 3 Section marched from Camp 14 to SUZANNE in relief of No 1 Section, No 1 Section having received orders to go into rest. Head Quarters & B Echelon moved from Camp 14 to BRAY preparatory to taking over the ammunition supply of the right section XV Corps front.	
BRAY	31st		During the month the following changes took place amongst officers.	
			Lt. W. J. DEACON joined No 3 Section for duty 1-12-16	
			" F. A. BRISCOE admitted to hospital 15-12-16	
			2/Lt F. R. PRICE struck off strength 8-12-16	
			" J. M. GLUCKSTEIN joined No 3 Section for duty 15-12-16	
			" J. G. ROYLE was admitted to hospital 21-12-16	
			Forty three men were admitted to hospital mainly belonging	

WAR DIARY
or
INTELLIGENCE SUMMARY.

Army Form C. 2118.

DECEMBER 16
Sheet 5.

Place	Date	Hour	Summary of Events and Information	Remarks and references to Appendices
BRAY			As "A" Echelon & in next came attributed to the extremely trying condition under which the ammunition supply was carried out. Workmen horses were exhausted. Trucks that a were destroyed. I of three were bullets to still fire or destroyed through jamming in shell holes. There were no casualties to officers or men from hostile shell fire.	

3.1.1917

[signature]
Comdg 4D [illegible]

Secret.

40th D.A.C.

Army Form C. 2118.

WAR DIARY
or
INTELLIGENCE SUMMARY.

JANUARY 17.

Instructions regarding War Diaries and Intelligence Summaries are contained in F.S. Regs., Part II. and the Staff Manual respectively. Title pages will be prepared in manuscript.

Vol 8

Place	Date	Hour	Summary of Events and Information	Remarks and references to Appendices
BRAY	1/1/17		The 40th D.A.C. took over from the 33rd D.A.C. 33rd D.A.C. remaining under the administration of the 40th D.A.C. Ammn supply was allotted as follows: No. 1 Section 40th D.A.C. supplied 151st Bde R.F.A. " 3 " " " 155th Bde R.F.A. " 1 " 33rd " 163rd Bde R.F.A. " 2 " " " 166th Bde R.F.A.	Ref. Albert continental sheet 1/40,000.
	4/1/17		The wagon lines of all Batteries were in the vicinity of SUZANNE No. 1 Section marched to VAUX-SUR-SOMME en-route to rest area at CONDE, accompanied by a detachment (9 G.S. wagons) of B Echelon.	Ref. Amiens sheet 17 1/100000
	5/1/17		No. 1 Section marched to LONGPRÉ	
	6/1/17		No. 1 Section marched to CONDE there to return the orders of 33rd Divnl Arty	
	6-1-17		The Command of the 40th Divnl Arty passed to Bar Genl C.H.W. Nickalls Rd.genl H.S. Reed V.C. C.M.G. having been appointed to command X Corps Artillery.	

WAR DIARY
or
INTELLIGENCE SUMMARY.
(Erase heading not required.)

Army Form C. 2118.

JANUARY 1917
(Sheet-2)

Place	Date	Hour	Summary of Events and Information	Remarks and references to Appendices
BRAY	8/1/17		Orders were received with reference to the re-organization of 40th Divisional Artillery into 2 bdes of 4 bty + a D.A.C. consisting of 2 sectns. The 188th Bde was disposed of as follows: A/188 became A/14 + joined 14th Bde RFA B/188 " A/5 " 5th " RFA C/188 joined A/14 " Corps Artillery D/188 transferred 1 section to D/171 making length Howitzer batteries. B/188 " " 1 " to C/188 6 gun batteries. No 2 Section D.A.C. was split up as follows: 4 G.S. Wagons, 24 other ranks 45 animals to 4.5 inch wagons Viis detachment was sent on the 10th instant. 4 G.S. Wagons to 5th Bde RFA 20 other ranks 40 horses, 6 15 pdr wagons to 14th " R+a 1 Officer (2nd Lt S.S. Walton R+a) 67 other ranks, 70 horses 6 15 pdr wagons 3 G.S. wagons + 1 water cart The above were handed over on the 14th January.	

WAR DIARY or INTELLIGENCE SUMMARY

JANUARY '17. Army Form C. 2118. (Sheet 3)

Place	Date	Hour	Summary of Events and Information	Remarks and references to Appendices
BRAY 8 & 14 Jan.			Owing to an outbreak of Stomatitis in No 2 section the men, animals & vehicles that had been posted to C/183 regiment in 2 section were again taken on the strength of the column. In addition all animals posted to the 5th Note N.Z.F.A. & the 14th Bde N.Z.F.A. were taken from B-echelon. B-echelon detached men to look after the animals of No 2 section will need time as they could be declared free from contagious disease. The following detail shows the composition of the force after reorganisation is completed. H.Q. & no change 216. Nos 1 & 2 Sections All ranks 272 animals. 15 Wagons ant. 15 pr. 6 wagon, rest 4.5. 11. G.S. wagons (3 in No 1) 7 wagon Limbers G.S. (5 in No 2) 1 Water cart. B-echelon 38 Other ranks 48 animals 7 wagons less than twelve of the total strength of the Column leaves 16 Officers 701 Other Ranks 796 Animals 136 Vehicles as against 15 Officers 834 Other Ranks	

Army Form C. 2118.

WAR DIARY
or
INTELLIGENCE SUMMARY.
(Erase heading not required.)

JANUARY '17. (Sheet 4.)

Place	Date	Hour	Summary of Events and Information	Remarks and references to Appendices
BRAY	14/1/17		1062 Animals 163 Vehicles. No 1 Section P⁰ D.A.C. came under the administration of the 4th D.A.C. to supply the 45th Div R.F.A. which came under 40th D.A. on the same date.	
	15/1/17		Nos 1 & 2 Section 33rd D.A.C. ceased to be administered by the 40th D.A.C. in consequence of the 162nd & 166th Bdes R.F.A. withdrawing from 40th Div. Arty. No 1 Section 40th D.A.C. & detachment Bleheim left CONDE for LONGPRE en route to SUZANNE.	
	16/1/17		No 1 Section marched to Camp 14 on CORBIE BRAY road 3½ miles W of BRAY.	
	17/1/17		No 1 Section rejoined the Clm at BRAY & took over supply of 17th Bde. No 2 Section was relieved & No 2 Section received to assist.	

WAR DIARY
or
INTELLIGENCE SUMMARY.

Army Form C. 2118.

JANUARY '17.
(Sheet 5)

Place	Date	Hour	Summary of Events and Information	Remarks and references to Appendices
BRAY			The system of supplying units in XV Corps area is as follows. Ammn is drawn from PLATEAU siding & delivered to an Advanced Refilling Point in L.19.d where batteries call for it. Owing to the condition of Bty animals due to exposure and hard work, much assistance has been given to Btys by their affiliated section D.A.C. Ammn was supplied to Btys as under. A 162 · 730 A/15 - 2939 A/31 · 3418 A/35 · 560 D 162 · 720 B · 1696 B · 2359 B · 835 A 166 · 376 C · 2005 C · 4154 C · 874 B 166 · 512 D · 1520 D · 2364 D · 432 D 166 · 697 8066 12189 2701 1st Bty 1210 3rd " 1716 Grand total 32,458 5th " 1644 of which 7,485 was 4.5 5th " 1852 9507	ALBERT Continued "/40 DD.

Army Form C. 2118.

WAR DIARY
or
INTELLIGENCE SUMMARY.
(Erase heading not required.)

January 17.
Sheet 6

Place	Date	Hour	Summary of Events and Information	Remarks and references to Appendices
BRAY			The following changes took place amongst the officers during Jan 17.	
			Capt. W. Parson to C/181. 2/Lt S.W. Baker to R.F.C. 2/Lt H.H. Stevens leave for England to his 2 station.	
			During the month nothing of a unusual in 'O' scheme was noted by the section concerned.	
	2-2-17			

Ay Brown.
LT. R.F.A.
ADJT. 40TH DIV. AMN. COL. R.F.A.

WAR DIARY
or
INTELLIGENCE SUMMARY

Army Form C. 2118.

FEBRUARY 1917

40th D.A.C.

Vol 9

Place	Date	Hour	Summary of Events and Information	Remarks and references to Appendices
BRAY	2/2/17		B Echelon organised as a small arm section were relieved by the S.A.A. section of D.A.C. at 10 a.m. & moved to VAUX-SUR-SOMME there to rest. To enable B Echelon to carry this S.A.A, all S.A. carts held by "A" Echelon were attached to them. Headquarters handed over to HQ 6th D.A.C. at the same time & removed in their rear quarters (File c.a.3 at rest)	Ref ALBERT sheet sheet 1/40000
	10/2/17		B Echelon returned to their former position in BRAY & took over duty from 6th D.A.C. at 8 a.m. 13th Feb. S.A.A. carts were returned to 'A' Echelon.	
	14/2/17		On the 15th Bde coming under the orders of 4th D.A. on the 12th a separate a/cs account was opened for the 4th given & the a/cts handled by No 2 Section.	
	22nd		In accordance with orders received from IV Army the following transfers took place on this unit having declared free from Scabies:	
			From No 1 Section 40th D.A.C. to 72nd D.A.C.	

Army Form C. 2118.

WAR DIARY
or
INTELLIGENCE SUMMARY.   Sheet II   FEBRUARY '17
(Erase heading not required.)

Instructions regarding War Diaries and Intelligence Summaries are contained in F. S. Regs., Part II. and the Staff Manual respectively. Title pages will be prepared in manuscript.

Place	Date	Hour	Summary of Events and Information	Remarks and references to Appendices
	4th			
BRAY	22		12 drivers & grooms & 24 horses & 4.5 wagons & 2 G.S. wagons. A similar detachment was transferred from No 2 section to the 242nd B.A.C.	
	25th		Lieut. E.P. Affma A.V.C. was transferred to IV Corps Heavy Artillery Capt. Gough A.V.C. took on veterinary charge of the Bde.
Guring the month all limbered G.S. wagons were exchanged with Infantry Battalion 4th Divn for S.A.A. carts. A great deal of assistance was given to Batteries by helping down the empty carts direct to gun positions.
The following units was delivered during the month 23421 rds 18 pdr 6134 4.5" 311 5.5
On the 25th February the D.A.C. was about of 84 other ranks and 123 animals	

WAR DIARY
or
INTELLIGENCE SUMMARY.

Army Form C. 2118.

Sheet III
February 17

Place	Date	Hour	Summary of Events and Information	Remarks and references to Appendices
BRAY	1-2-17		No 42511 Dr E Straw died on 16-2-17 of Broncho-Pneumonia at 21 C.C.S.	

A Dunphy

Army Form C. 2118

WAR DIARY
INTELLIGENCE SUMMARY
40th D.A.C. R. & A.
MARCH 1917 (sheet 1)

Maps: 1/40,000 AMIENS 17 1/100,000
ALBERT continued 1/40,000

Place	Date	Hour	Summary of Events and Information	Remarks and references to Appendices
BRAY	March 9th 10		In consequence of a re-adjustment of the XV Corps front the 45th Bde R.F.A ceased to be administered by the 40th Divl Arty & the 14th Army Field Artillery Bde was attached. The 14th R.A.C came under the orders of 40th D.A.C. Wagon lines of 40th Divn Batteries moved from Cant 21 as under. A 176 G.11.d.4.4 B } G.11.d.5.5 C } D } A 151 B } C } G 10 central D } 65th 68th } A 14 8th G.16.a.9.5 14th B.A.C moved from L.4.d to G.13.b.3.5. Section of 40th D.A.C. remained in same position HQ 40th D.A.C moved to P.C.6 L.15.a.0.7 The A.R.P at B.19.d was handed over to 5th D.A. + a new one at H.7.c.3.5 taken over by 2/Sr Wanwick from 33rd D.A.	

WAR DIARY
INTELLIGENCE SUMMARY

(Erase heading not required.)

MARCH 1917 (Sheet II)

Army Form C. 2118

Place	Date	Hour	Summary of Events and Information	Remarks and references to Appendices
P.C. 6. L15.a.07	15th		Warning orders were received with reference to action to be taken in the event of voluntary withdrawal on the part of the enemy.	Order No 31
	16th		A new A.R.P. was formed at H5c and filled with mules withdrawn from gun positions rendered vacant by the advance of 40th D.A. batteries	
	21/M/23		The 14th Army Field Artillery Pool withdrew from 40th D.A + the 14th R.A.P. ceased to be administered by 40th D.A.C.	Order No 33
	22nd		On formation of a mobile column the Bgde furnished 4. 18 pdr Q.F. wagons + 2 G.S. wagons carrying 76,000 rds S.A.A. This detachment unit consisted of 2/Smith, 9 Thorpe moved to HAUT ALLAINES + came under command of by O.C. 119th Bty. Bde.	Order No 29
	26th		The XV Corps was re-constituted as follows: 5th, 20th + 40th Divns. with 40th Divn (less Artillery) in Corps reserve. No 1 section 40th D.A.C. came under 20th D.A. at 2 p.m. 27th + moved to COMBLES on same date. No 2 Section came under 5th D.A at some time + date but remained in old position.	
	27th		B Echelon moved to VAUX.	

Army Form C. 2118

WAR DIARY
or
INTELLIGENCE SUMMARY

(Erase heading not required.)

MARCH 1917 (Sheet III)

Place	Date	Hour	Summary of Events and Information	Remarks and references to Appendices
PC 6 Libad	27th		To enable the 17th Bde to move to its new divisional area the Bde furnished 2 6 hour teams which were retained on completion of duty.	N.A. Order No 40
	26th		The mobile detachment under 2nd Lt Thorne rejoined the Bde on the evacuation of the mobile column	no 41
	31st		A warning order was received to the effect that 2 Bdes of 4 Div Arty would come into the line between 2 pm & 9 pm on after 3rd April.	no 42

Ammunition

	A	B	C	D
A	4178	3274		
		2792		
		1642		
		1091		
				1093

	A	B	C	D
A	4151	3215		
		4907		
		933		
		788		
				10196

Ammunition was supplied as follows during March

	65th	78th	A/14	1st Bde	20th DA	7 DA
				13885	300	1636
				2523	152	3253
				1791	677	
	1765					

Totals: 7299, 1079, 4889

Total 25,552 to which 4 256 was 4.5 shrapnel anti gas rounds 15 amnd. all amn in reserve gun position was taken over by the BAC. The total amn. taken over being 9631 shell 15 shr + 7602 cart. 4.5

In addition 15 .303 ball

Army Form C. 2118

WAR DIARY
or
INTELLIGENCE SUMMARY
(Erase heading not required.)

MARCH 1917 (Sheet-IV)

Place	Date	Hour	Summary of Events and Information	Remarks and references to Appendices
PC 6 L15a07	[n.d.]		On 25th inst: 78 horses + 32 mules were drawn from railhead at CERISY + on 28th instant a further 144 horses were taken at the same place. In order to ease remount horses from long put into heavy work with the gun animals were transferred as follows. No 1 Section transferred 106 fit-horses to 178th Bde. + received 108 mules from B Echelon. No 2 Section transferred 104 fit-horses + 36 mules (with their drivers) to 181st Bde. + receiving 148 mules from B Echelon. B Echelon took over the 216 remount-horses + 32 remount-mules. This transaction was completed on 31st March. From the 15th instant the D.A.C. furnished 30 G.S. wagons per road repair work under the XV Corps remount officer. These were found pro rata by sections until the 23rd instant when they were found by B Echelon entirely + detached or follow-up at MAUREPAS remain under O/C Cruden to whom is	

WAR DIARY
or
INTELLIGENCE SUMMARY

Army Form C. 2118 (Sheet I)

MARCH 1917

Place	Date	Hour	Summary of Events and Information	Remarks and references to Appendices
P&G LIDAO7	General		vicinity of COMBLES LE FOREST + RANCOURT and the works St Walliers at work under O.C. 40th Divl Works Ptn in vicinity of CURLU.	
	7.3.17		No 2 Section assisted the 151st Pnr R.T.a. with teams on 7 occasions to enable them to carry out moves, the R.T.a. being short of horses. The following casualties affecting officers occurred during the month.	
			Capt M Fitzgerald 5th Dragoon Guards (R.O.) goes for duty in connection with care of horses + was attached to H.Q.	
	17.3.17		2/Sr. R.G. Sage joined from 2nd Divn on appointment as a munition Learner in the field.	
	18.3.17		2/Sr. W.G. Beacon was posted to C/181st Bde R.T.a. 2/Sr. Y. Bragg was posted to 40th Bde in exchange. Why above exchange was held in abeyance pending further instructions	
	21.3.17		2/Lieut + y. Servir was struck of strength of Column on appointment to the R.F.C.	

Army Form C. 2118

WAR DIARY
or
INTELLIGENCE SUMMARY
(Erase heading not required.)

MARCH 1917 Sheet VI

Place	Date	Hour	Summary of Events and Information	Remarks and references to Appendices
PC 4 L16a07			Seventeen O.R. + 9 horses were evacuated during the month. 4th Column received reinforcements to complete establishment + on the 31st March was up to strength in men.	

1-4-17

A.E. Dempsey
Lt Col R.t.a.
Commdg 40th B.C.e. R.t.a

Army Form C. 2118

Sheet 62c
57c
A439
3/5/17

40th Div

WAR DIARY
or
INTELLIGENCE SUMMARY
(Erase heading not required.)

APRIL '17 Sheet I

Vol XI

Place	Date April	Hour	Summary of Events and Information	Remarks and references to Appendices
PC w L'taoy	5th		B Echelon moved to CLERY (H.S.C.) close to site of old ARP. All wagons & teams away in XIV Corps roadwork rejourney.	
	6th		A new ARP was established under "Saint of Ramonfucia" at FINS.	
	7th		HQ + A Echelon moved to MOISLAINS and VAUX WOOD (C6a) respectively.	
	21st		15 S A A carts complete with drivers and animals were handed over from A Echelon to the E road to Infantry Bde of 40th Division. In consequence of above the mobile establishment of S A A at A Echelon B Echelon became as follows	and the

S A A
carried by wagons
600,000
0414

0331
680,000
15 Echelon

WAR DIARY
INTELLIGENCE SUMMARY

4th D.A.C.
APRIL 1917 Sheet II

Place	Date	Hour	Summary of Events and Information	Remarks and references to Appendices
MOISLAINS	21st		Following amounts of 3" Stokes Trench Mortar Ammunition were ordered to the mobile equipment. A Echelon 630 rds B Echelon 720 rds.	
	26th		A Echelon less Heavy Section moved to vicinity of MANANCOURT No 1 Section V.19.d.73 No 2 Section V.19.b.53	
MANANCOURT	28th		H.Q. moved to E. of MANANCOURT V.13.d.36. During the month the following amounts of ammunition were salved from the old gun positions in vicinity of CLERY. 9040 rds 18 pdr 7602 rds 4.5. Ammunition was issued as follows:- A 9115 5171 a 317 1427 1st SAA 608 grand total B 3520 B 577 3rd 304 37795 C 3412 C 3340 5th 144 of which 5905 D 2749 D 313 1056 were 4.5 total 18,796 2159	

WAR DIARY
INTELLIGENCE SUMMARY

Army Form C. 2118
APRIL — Sheet 3

Place	Date	Hour	Summary of Events and Information	Remarks and references to Appendices
MANAN COURT			On the 24th instant 9600 rds were issued to batteries this being the largest amount of ammunition issued from the echelon in one day to date. In addition to the above the following approximate amounts of ammunition were salved from the vicinity of CLERY + delivered to FINS by B echelon. S.A.A. 1,25,000. 3" stokes 3750. No 5 grenades 22,500. Very lights 5400 and a quantity of flares rockets etc. The Colony continued to assist the batteries with teams + horses for ammunition supply. The following changes of establishment occurred during April. 2/Lt J.R. Benningfield joined 2-4-17 + was posted to B echelon. 2/Lts J Parker + R.C. Ashurn joined 10-4-17 + were posted to B echelon + HQ respectively.	

Army Form C. 2118

WAR DIARY
or
INTELLIGENCE SUMMARY
(Erase heading not required.)

April Sheet 4

Place	Date	Hour	Summary of Events and Information	Remarks and references to Appendices
NANANCOURT			2/Lt. S. H. Pelham joined on first appointment 13-4-17. Ab nos Section. 2/Lt E Elliott & Lt Arell joined 29th April & were posted to no 2 & 1 Section respectively. Lieut. W. Parsons (D.O) M.O. joined 30-4-17 & was posted to B Section. Lieut Col A S Smoly admitted to hurricase 10-4-17. 2/Lt. H. a Yeldon - Joined 17th Bde 10-4-17. 2/Lt. R. D. Sayer to 181st Bde 23-4-17. S/S. Archer to 181st Bde 28-4-17. Two drafts of remounts were received in the column during the month. 165 on the 29th, 140 of which were horses on the 13ees & 133 on the 30th, 90 of which were horses on the 13ees. Twenty-seven other ranks were evacuated & a draft of 3-5-17	

Army Form C. 2118

No. 4638
Date 6/6/17
R.F.A.

WAR DIARY
INTELLIGENCE SUMMARY

40th Div. R.F.A.
May 1917

Sheet 1
Reference Sheets 62c
57s

Place	Date	Hour	Summary of Events and Information	Remarks and references to Appendices
MANANCOURT	5th May		B Echelon moved from CLERY (H.5.c) to BOIS DE VAUX U.29.c	
	6th		Lieut Col R.N. Stewart R.t.a. (T.F.) assumed command of 40th D.A.C. 1st Section 1st D.A.C. moved from the area + reported to be attached to 40th D.A.C.	
	15th		Owing to the withdrawal of the 5th Division ammunition dumps were taken over from the 5th D.A.C. which now cleared of 6000 rounds 18 pr + 2700 rounds 4.5 which was dumped at A.R.P. FINS.	
	21st		A further 3600 rounds were taken over from the 5th D.A.C. and cleared + tidied + handed over to the 35th D.A.C. on the 25th May.	
			The following ammunition was issued to Btys during May:	
			A 178 5007 A 181 7179 113th Bty 4689 Total 65443
			B " 8181 B " 6740 114th " 4627 of which 9934
			C " 7602 C " 7076 115th " 2808 rds were 4.5.
			D " 3952 D " 3040 40th " 2942
			Total 24742 Total 24035 16066

WAR DIARY
or
INTELLIGENCE SUMMARY

Army Form C. 2118

May 17

Place	Date	Hour	Summary of Events and Information	Remarks and references to Appendices
MANANCOURT	May		169 teams were finished to various batteries during May.	
			The following changes affecting officers occurred during the month.	
			2nd Lt. A. Elliott transferred to 181st Bde 3.5.17	
			" " A.J. Sevier joined for duty 20.5.17	
			" " V.A. Blunden " " 22.5.17	
			" " Reg Rees " " 22.5.17	
			" " H.W. Briggs struck of strength 23.5.17	
			" " R.C. Ashton transferred 181st Bde 24.5.17	
			" " J.G. Pelham " " 24.5.17	
	3-6-17			

R.P. Stewart
LT-COLONEL, R.F.A.
COMDG. 40th DIV. AMN. COL. R.F.A.

Army Form C. 2118

WAR DIARY
or
INTELLIGENCE SUMMARY

4 GROUP HAC

June July 1917 Sheet I

Ref. Sheets 62c + 57c 1/40000

Vol 13

Place	Date	Hour	Summary of Events and Information	Remarks and references to Appendices
MANANCOURT	1st		The 40th Division came under the III rd Corps which relieved the XV Corps on this date. A new A.R.P. at W.3.c.2.9 was commenced under the supervision of 2/Lt. W.G. Neacroft & a party of men from the D.A.C. Working parties were found nightly to assist — in accordance with the plan two weeks + on the 30th June the dump was practically completed.	
	2nd		Put of 6 men per battery were furnished from the D.A.C. to assist in the preparation of gun positions there now to turned to the D.A.C. on the 30th June. The following ammunition was issued to Batteries during June A 175 2052 B " 1542 C " 3108 D " 1691 8493 A 181 2324 B " 2476 C " 4470 D " 1701 11170 Total 19,602 of which 3648 were L.S.	

WAR DIARY
or
INTELLIGENCE SUMMARY

Army Form C. 2118

June 1917 (2nd Sheet)

Place	Date	Hour	Summary of Events and Information	Remarks and references to Appendices
MANCOURT	June		The following changes affecting officers occurred during June Lt H.L. WEBBER posted to 181st Bde 2-6-17 2Lt S J WRIGHT posted to 181st Bde 9-6-17 Lt F BARKER evacuated to England 1-6-17 (sick now) No 1252 Sergeant J Moores was mentioned in despatches for devotion to duty. Seventy remount mules were received during June reducing the deficiency of animals in the Bde to 71. 4-7-17	

R.R. Stewart
Lt. Colonel, R.F.A.
Commanding 180th Bde, R.F.A.

WAR DIARY
or
INTELLIGENCE SUMMARY

Army Form C. 2118

40th D.A.C. R.T.A. Sheet 1

July 1917. Vol 14

Ref sheets 62c + 57c. 1/40000

Place	Date	Hour	Summary of Events and Information	Remarks and references to Appendices
MANANCOURT	3rd		No 2 Section 35th D.A.C. came under orders of 40th D.A.C. to supply 159th Hav. R.T.A. with ammunition. The A R P at 35th Division at W.16.A. was taken over by the 40th D.A.C.	
	6th		No 2 Section 35th D.A.C. rejoined 35th D.A.C.	
	8th		The A R P at FINS was closed and the new ARP at W.3.c. opened for issue, the ARP at W.16.a. being retained for storage of defective ammunition pending return to Corps Ammunition Park. No 2 Section 59th D.A.C. came under orders of 40th D.A.C. to supply the 296th Hav. R.T.A. with ammunition	
NURLU	10th		The 40th D.A.C. moved from vicinity of MANANCOURT to NURLU and took up positions as follows with a view to informing units starting P.T.O.	

Army Form C. 2118

WAR DIARY 40th Div July 17
INTELLIGENCE SUMMARY Sheet II
(Erase heading not required.)

Place	Date	Hour	Summary of Events and Information	Remarks and references to Appendices
NURLU	July 17		HQ V.25.d.4.4 No 1 Section V.25.c.9.1 No 2 Section V.23.c.8.3	
			B. Echelon V.25.d.6.5. No 2 Section 5.9.B Pierre D.10.a. (Sheet 62c)	
			Ammunition used is as follows during July:	
			1st period (151 Rds)	
			A 931 A 3818 A 9501 A 1741	
			B 1702 B 784 B 9056 B 5111	
			C 1449 C 2775 C 9501 C 2142	
			D 591 D 1831 D 399 D 3051	
			────── ────── ────── ──────	
			5693 (?) 7578 3816 9177	
			A great deal of Stokes mort. was furnished by the Bde	
			beyond total 26,916 of which 5,460 rounds	
			to assist the 148th Brigade Coy, 178th Bn Rifle, 151st	
			Bde N+a III Corps mortar officer etc.	

Army Form C. 2118
Sheet III

WAR DIARY
or
INTELLIGENCE SUMMARY
(Erase heading not required.)

July 17

Place	Date	Hour	Summary of Events and Information	Remarks and references to Appendices
NURLU	July		The following changes affecting Officers occurred during the month. Lt. Col. A.S. Dunlop struck off strength 4-7-17. 2/Lt. A. Sinclair joined & re section for duty 9-7-17. 2/Lt. V.R. Rumsell posted to 178th Bde A.T. 9-7-17.	

Stuff, Capt. N.T.a
Comg 87th Coy D.O.E. N.T.a

3-3-17

40th D.A.C. R.T.A.

WAR DIARY

August 1917. Army Form C. 2118

Ref 1/40,000 Sheet 57c
6 2 c.

INTELLIGENCE SUMMARY

(Erase heading not required.)

Instructions regarding War Diaries and Intelligence Summaries are contained in F. S. Regs., Part II. and the Staff Manual respectively. Title Pages will be prepared in manuscript.

Place	Date	Hour	Summary of Events and Information	Remarks and references to Appendices
NURLU	2nd		No 2 Section 54th D.A.C. moved to VILLIERS FAUCON to form 3rd Army No 2 Section. 58th D.A.C. were attached for duty to supply 241st Bde R.F.A.	
	5th		No 2 Section 58th D.A.C. ceased to be attached for duty. No 2 42nd D.A.C. were attached for duty to supply No 2 211 Bde R.F.A.	
	16th		The Establishment of the D.A.C. was altered & reorganisation as follows. "A" Echelon ceased to carry small arm ammunition + bombs. "B" Echelon became the S.A.A. section. The small arm ammunition S.A.A. wagons in detachment with Infantry Brigades rejoined the column + were transferred to the S.A.A. Section. In consequence of the re-organisation 1 g.s. wagon from No 1 Section + 17 from the S.A.A. section together with 1 maltese cart were transferred to join the Divisional Ammunition Park at MOISLAINS	

WAR DIARY or INTELLIGENCE SUMMARY

Army Form C. 2118
August 1917
2nd Sheet

Place	Date	Hour	Summary of Events and Information	Remarks and references to Appendices
NURLU	16th		Depot at ABBEVILLE. The surplus personnel were sent to the base on 30th following view the difference in establishment.	
			Original estab. Riding horses Sight-draught Q.F. wagons G.S. wagons L.G.S.	
			Officers O.R.	
			15 1395 699 — — — 15	
			newly 15 505 76 913 37 15	
			No 2 Section H.Q. and S.O.E. ceased to be attached for duty.	
	22nd		Ammunition formation during the month were as follows.	
			A 178 1395 A 151 1114 A 211 456 A 296 456	
			B 2452 B 1271 B — B 225	
			C 1330 C 1900 C 364 C 632	
			D 371 D 395 D 372 D 576	
			Total 5969 6753 1197 1892	
			Grand total 16,307 of which 14,654 were S.A.A.	

WAR DIARY
or
INTELLIGENCE SUMMARY

Army Form C. 2118

August 17   3rd Sheet

Place	Date	Hour	Summary of Events and Information	Remarks and references to Appendices
NURLU	August		2/Lieut S.C. Jenkins joined for duty 7-8-17. 2/Lieut J.V. Bromfield (SR) posted to 178th Bde 7-8-17. The whole of the men in the Column were inspected by a Corps committee with a view to selecting suitable men + 26 men were selected + branded.	
	31-8-17			

R.R. Cumins'
Lieut Col. R.F.A.
Cmdg 40th F.A.E. R.F.A.

Army Form C. 2118

WAR DIARY 40th Div. A.T.A.
or
INTELLIGENCE SUMMARY
(Erase heading not required.)

September 1917

Ref ¼0,000 Sheets 62c
57c

JA/16

Place	Date	Hour	Summary of Events and Information	Remarks and references to Appendices

NURLU	September		During the month 65 wagons were furnished to assist the Corps Personal Officers – Divisional Engineers – Tunnelling Company & 239 A.T. Coy R.E. An average of 45 wagons daily were furnished. Winter camps were completed during the month as far as material was available. Output was never during the month as follows:
			
			A 1678 1536
			B 1673 565
			C 1678 309
			D 1678 1951
			           4297
			
			A 131 1947
			B 131 1970
			C 131 1352
			D 131 1947
			      5192
			
			Total output of whole of 2120 new
			
			L.S.
			
			The following changes affecting officers took place during the month	

WAR DIARY
or
INTELLIGENCE SUMMARY

(Erase heading not required.)

Army Form C. 2118

Place	Date	Hour	Summary of Events and Information	Remarks and references to Appendices

Lieut. H. a. H. Sleight joined 2-9-17 posted to 178th Bde 10-9-17
2/Lt S.C. Salsbury posted to 178th Bde 7-7-17
St. a.e. Henderson joined 21-9-17
St J Thorpe posted to 178th Bde 25-9-17

3 – 10 – 17

Hall Capt R.F.A.
for Lt Col R.F.A. Cmdg 40th Div Arty

Secret

Reference: LENS 11 Army Form C. 2118.
ST QUENTIN 15 1/10,000

WAR DIARY
or
INTELLIGENCE SUMMARY

40th D.A.C. H.Q.

October 1917

Place	Date	Hour	Summary of Events and Information	Remarks and references to Appendices
NURLU	4/10/17		Orders received for the S.A.A. section to join the 40th Divn Infantry to move by march route in the vicinity of MONCHIET on the 10th October	
"	7/10/17		March of S.A.A. section cancelled.	
"	25/10/17		Orders received for the 40th D.A.C. 20th D.A.C. + move to 5th Army area by train. 40th D.A.C. handed over to 20th D.A.C. at 10 a.m.	
"	26/10/17		The D.A.C. was to move in #1 Trains as under:— Train No 1 section of No1 section } Train Hennevort remainder of No 1 " } at 4 hour intervals 3 section of No 5 " } commencing 5 " " " 7 " at 11 am & 7pm 9 " " "	

Army Form C. 2118.

WAR DIARY
or
INTELLIGENCE SUMMARY.
(Erase heading not required.)

Sheet II

Place	Date	Hour	Summary of Events and Information	Remarks and references to Appendices
MURLU 17th			Train No 2 {Parties of No 2 Section Remainder of No 2 " " " Portion of " " } CHAPELLETTE at ½ hour intervals commencing 1 — 4 of 27	
			" No 4	
			" " 3	
			" " 9	
			" " 10	
			" No 11 } Head quarters 4 ½ Section FLAMICOURT 7 pm (28th)
			12 ½ SAA Section CHAPPELLETTE 9 am
			13 " " " FLAMICOURT 11 am
			The move had commenced & train No 1 & 2 had already started when the move was cancelled & instructions received orders to move its contents under No 1 Section ST DENIS CORNER
			9 " CHAPELLETTE
			PERONNE — DOINGT RD
			SAA with SAA Section
			HQ " " "	

Army Form C. 2118.

WAR DIARY
or
INTELLIGENCE SUMMARY.

(Erase heading not required.)

Sheet III

Place	Date	Hour	Summary of Events and Information	Remarks and references to Appendices
PERONNE	31st		Orders received for 40th DAC to return to NURLU	
			Ammunition was issued as under during October	
			A 176 1784 A 181 1630	
			B 1754 B 1520	
			C 1756 C 3400	
			D 1210 D 852	
			_____ _____	
			6496 7432	
			Rgmt total 13930	
			of which 2092 was L.5.	
			There were no changes affecting officers during the month.	

R.R.Maurice
O.C. 40th DIV. AMM. COLUMN.

Army Form C. 2118.

WAR DIARY 40th D.A.C. N^ta.

INTELLIGENCE SUMMARY.

December   Ref. Sheets 57c & 57b
1/40,000

Place	Date Dec	Hour	Summary of Events and Information	Remarks and references to Appendices
TRES CAULT	1st		The D.A.C. remained encamped at TRESCAULT under 47th D.A. with ants dump on decauville railway 400 yards W. of the village.	
	3rd		The S.A.A. Section moved to BERTINCOURT.	
K17d	5th		In anticipation of the Evacuation of BOURLON wood the D.A.C. less S.A.A. Section moved to a camp on the METZ–BERTINCOURT road at K17d. Whilst column evacuating from a vacated gun portion of C/131st Bde No 2 Section lost 3 men killed & 1 wounded. Before leaving TRESCAULT a flight of enemy aeroplanes strafed 15 horses in the vicinity of the D.A.C. camp killing 2 men & 7 horses & wounding 4 men & 12 horses.	
BERTIN COURT	9th		The D.A.C. moved to BERTINCOURT.	
	10th		The Anti refilling point at TRESCAULT was handed over to 62 D.A.C.	
	12th		The 40th Divl Arty moved to HAMELINCOURT & went into quarters vacated by the 16th D.A.C. who proceeded	

Army Form C. 2118.

WAR DIARY
INTELLIGENCE SUMMARY.
(Erase heading not required.)

Jan. 17
Sheet 2

Place	Date	Hour	Summary of Events and Information	Remarks and references to Appendices
HAMELIN COURT	12th		for all roads. The 178th + 151st Btys moved straight into action + the B.A.C. supplied gun positions direct with a quantity of entrenching tools at gun dumps on the nights 12th/13th + 13th/14th.	
	9pm	The 16th B.Cie marched out to join the 16th Divn. + the 40th moved into the vacated camps, which were well erected + gave sufficient + good accommodation for all ranks + all animals. Sections were located as follows:- H Q + No 1 Section S.25.d.9.1. No 2 Section S.29.d.4.9. S.A.A. Section S.30.c.1.6. A.R.P. T.19.c.5.5. During the month the B.A.C. supplied reinforcements to the extent of 160 other ranks to the 178th + 131st Bdes + by 25th instant reinforcements had been received from the Base which made the Unit up to strength. In addition 150 horses were handed in to Remount & Detail to make up casualties.	

Army Form C. 2118.

WAR DIARY
or
INTELLIGENCE SUMMARY.
(Erase heading not required.)

Dec. 17
Sheet 3.

Place	Date	Hour	Summary of Events and Information	Remarks and references to Appendices
HAMELIN-COURT	Dec. 17		+ On 31st Dec the D.O.C was 24 rounds short of estab.	
			Honours + Rewards	
			Capt J. Yeall mentioned in despatches London Gazette 11/12/17	
			From S.S. Provenum NoSec. "	
			Military Medal	
			Sergeant J. Moores SAA Section Divnl. Routine Orders of. 20/12/17.	
			Casualties	
			Killed in Action	
			90139 Cpl. SS Moulam W.R.	
			42625 Pr. Bradley W	
			35742 " Lomos D. W. Cof	
			65919 " Walker C.J.B	
			Changes in Officers. Lieut. T.J. Lewin to T.M.B's 15-12-17	
			B. J. Plow to SAA Section 15-12-17	
			to no. Section 20-12-17	
			B. O Whelder to rel. Section 20-12-17	
			A. C. Henderson from A to SAA Sec 26/12/17	

WAR DIARY
or
INTELLIGENCE SUMMARY.
(Erase heading not required.)

Army Form C. 2118.

Dec 14 Sheet 4

Place	Date	Hour	Summary of Events and Information	Remarks and references to Appendices
			Ammunition used.	
			During December ammunition was issued as under	
			18 pdr 40260 4.5 6762	
			Lethal 500.	
			Grand total 47522	
			W.R Renwick	
			Captain N+a	
			C.m.d.g 40th Bde R.F.a	

WAR DIARY or INTELLIGENCE SUMMARY

Army Form C. 2118

Pt Sheet 51 b } 1/40,000
57 c } P.O.C.
LENS " 1/10,000
Sheet I

Vol 20

Place	Date	Hour	Summary of Events and Information	Remarks and references to Appendices
HAMELINCOURT	Jan 15		144 trained other ranks under Lieut. G. Ellison joined the 40th B.O.C. for duty in accordance with a new establishment authorised for certain B.O.C. These men who were only partially trained are being home [intensively?] to the establishment for the time being. Duplicates of them were detailed to hospital during January. Military medals were awarded as follows during January: 57403 Cpl. J. Jeavons, 68644 " Sjnr. W. [Davis?], 1951 Sm. Sgt. [Scotgem?], 35773 Pr. [Brudin?], 44781 " L.A. Manning. Casualties 1 O.R. died of wounds, 2 O.R. wounded.	

WAR DIARY
or
INTELLIGENCE SUMMARY
(Erase heading not required.)

Army Form C. 2118

Sheet - II
Jan. '18

Changes affecting Officers.

LIEUT G. COLLINSON R.F.A.(T) Joined SAA Section 5-1-18.
(T) A. SIMKINS R.F.A Posted to B/181st Bde 23-1-18.
"LIEUT W. HAINING R.F.A. (S.R.) Joined No 2 Section 24-1-18.

Ammunition.
The following rounds were received & issued during
January 15,134 18,190 7,766 4.5.

R.F. Elements
Lt-Col R.F.A.
Comdg 40th D.A. R.F.A.

3/2/18

40th DAC

WAR DIARY or INTELLIGENCE SUMMARY

Army Form C. 2118.

40th DAC R.F.A.
Ref Sheet 51.G 1/40000
Zone 11 M/40000

Vol 27

Place	Date	Hour	Summary of Events and Information	Remarks and references to Appendices
HAMELINCOURT	February		The Command of the DAC came under the authority of the 34th Bde. on the 13th February 18. The Ammn Column Section came under orders of the 3rd Divisional Arty on 9th February 1918. On 7th February 18 a warning order to move was received. During the month the following Officers went forces to the Column. 9/Lt E.W. Toyton to No. 1 Section 15/2/18, 2/Lt J.S. Hampton to No. 1 Section 20/2/18. 2/Lt am Sergeant O.G. Brown were evacuated to England sick/aft strength 10/2/18. Ammunition. The following ammunition was issued to Batteries during February. 18 pr 29,166 4.5 how 6,272 Chemical 1430. Casualties 1 man wounded by bomb from hostile aircraft 17/2/18. Names: Gnr 33799 B.S.M. Quedar W.J. S.A.A. ddon (L1035) B.S.M. Wildman J.G. lost 1 sling lost lanyard on arrival the Belgian horses in ppe ?	

R.R. Allison
Comdg 40th DAC R.F.A.

Confidential

Army Form C. 2118.

40th Bde R.F.A.
Ref sheets 51b, 51c, 57D
Zone II

WAR DIARY
or
INTELLIGENCE SUMMARY.
(Erase heading not required.)

Place	Date	Hour	Summary of Events and Information	Remarks and references to Appendices
HAMELINCOURT	1/3/18		J.O.L. moved to 6th Corps Reserve & were relocated: HQ & Bdy 1 & 2 Echelons at Gaudienpre D2c, SAA &c at Borgneuse J9a.	
	11/3/18		Moved to above reserve. Relocated at Bours St. Martin S14a.	
	25/3/18		In consequence of the withdrawal of the line the following moves took place.	
	25/3/18		To AYETTE - BUCQUOY to F15 b	
	25/3/18		To MONCHY au BOIS F1 d	
	26/3/18		To SIMENCOURT Q11 c	
	31/3/18		HQ No 1 & 2 Sec came under orders of Generals & 3rd D.A. respectively for ammunition supply. No 3 Sec moved to BRETENCOURT	
			SAA station.	
	21/3/18		Came under orders of 40th Reserve G	
	29/3/18		Reformed DAC at SIMENCOURT	
	29/3/18		Bonnecourt Ammunition Dump taken over by S.O.L. The dump was worked until the 29/3/18	

Army Form C. 2118.

WAR DIARY
or
INTELLIGENCE SUMMARY.
(Erase heading not required.)

Instructions regarding War Diaries and Intelligence Summaries are contained in F. S. Regs., Part II. and the Staff Manual respectively. Title pages will be prepared in manuscript.

Place	Date	Hour	Summary of Events and Information	Remarks and references to Appendices

Ammunition

The following ammunition was issued by the DAC during the month

18 pdr	H.E. how
8733 rds	2448 rds

Officers

The undermentioned have joined during the month

2/Lt T.H. Tate — Posted to SAA Section
2/Lt P.H. Saul — Attached to No 1 Section
2/Lt T.J. Bath — " " No 2 "
2/Lt A.J. Rutland — " " SAA "

2/Lt B.F. Bliss was transferred to 1st Corps as Corps Agricultural Officer & struck off strength 19/3/18

The following reinforcements have been supplied to Brigades

175th Bde R.F.A.	1 S.S. 2 Bdrs 8 Gunners 6 Drivers
151st Bde R.F.A.	30 L.D. animals

R.P. Oliviar
Lt Col. R.F.A.
Commandy 11th Divl Arml Amtn Colm R.F.A.

Confidential

40th D.A.C. R.F.A.

WAR DIARY
or
INTELLIGENCE SUMMARY.

Army Form C. 2118.

Ref sheet 31st 1/40,000

Vol 24

Place	Date	Hour	Summary of Events and Information	Remarks and references to Appendices
ETRLES au Bois	14/5/18		In consequence of the relief of the 40th Divisional Artillery the 40th D.A.C. moved to SAULTY while in reserve training was proceeded with on the following programme:— Marching & Physical drill Gas drill Riding School for Natives Troops Driving drills	40th Divl. City Order No. 135
SAULTY	30/5/18		The 40th D.A.C. relieved the 31st D.A.C. & moved to Gaudiempre V26c 5A 2/Lt D.S. Kempton with a party of 4 other ranks took over the ARP at D6 & 6.5 As a means of defence against enemy cavalry a party of men under an officer of each section are nearing several instructions in manning ten the making of barricades The S.A.A. Section 40th D.A.C. was disbanded during the month under orders of the 3rd Army, the following officers of that section struck off strength Capt J. Hole 2/Lt J. Coleman 2/Lt A.C. Henderson 2/Lt B.T. Shillabut 2/Lt T. Thorpe	40th Divl. City Order No. 156 BM/9/2

Army Form C. 2118.

WAR DIARY
or
INTELLIGENCE SUMMARY.
(Erase heading not required.)

Instructions regarding War Diaries and Intelligence Summaries are contained in F. S. Regs., Part II. and the Staff Manual respectively. Title pages will be prepared in manuscript.

Place	Date	Hour	Summary of Events and Information	Remarks and references to Appendices
GAUDIEHPRE			The following awards have been made to officers & 60 men of S.A.A. Section during the month	
			Lt T Thorpe Military Cross	
			No 36743 B.Q.M.S. Adams L Military Medal	
			4190 Sgt Milton T "	
			46074 Cpl Robertson A "	
			47053 " Barclay J "	
			34568 " Baton J "	
			39994 " Harper G "	
			630730 " McKenzie L. R.E. "	
			46699 " Isaac L.B. "	
			44385 " Clegg F "	
			43814 " Sutton E "	
			7736 " Harwell E "	
			80143 " Wordsworth "	
			Lt B.F Bloon (T.F) was posted to the D.A.C from 1st Corps & taken on strength 24/5/18	
			Casualties during the month NIL	

R.N. Stewart
LT COLONEL R.E.

Confidential

SECRET

40th Divl Anti Column R.F.A.

WAR DIARY or INTELLIGENCE SUMMARY

Army Form C. 2118.

Refuted 51º / 49,000

(Erase heading not required.)

Place	Date	Hour	Summary of Events and Information	Remarks and references to Appendices
GAUDIECHART	20/6/18		**RELIEFS** The 2nd Divl Arty relieved the 40th Divl Arty. The Brigades will take over the districts taken of the D.A.C. moving strength into actn. As i/c are commanded details of the 3rd Divl Arty relieves No 1 Section 39th D.A.C. of Q15a No 2 the com under details of the 2nd Canadian Div relieves the 15th B.A.C. at Q14 Headquarters D.A.C. moved to P16a 3.4 22/6/18	40th Divl Arty Order No 141
	22/6/18		**INSPECTION** The nature of arrival of the BAC was inspected by Lieut Gen Sir E. Cecil, K.C.B., D.S.O.	
			OFFICERS The following postings of Officers occurred during the month Lt T/Lieut MC posted to No 1 Sec 11/6/18 from R H.K.T.Q. Base Depot 2/Lt BS Leeke posted to No 1 Sec 26/4/18 3/Lt JA Horton posted to No 2 Sec 11/6/18 ... from No 1 A.A. Battery Wearing transferred to 51st Div area 2/Lt ... posted to No 2 Sec 15/6/18 Lt BFDixon admitted to hospital invalided by No 30 MAC 11/6/18 Evacuated to 40th Divl T.M. Battn 23/6/18	

Army Form C. 2118.

WAR DIARY
or
INTELLIGENCE SUMMARY.
(Erase heading not required.)

Place	Date	Hour	Summary of Events and Information	Remarks and references to Appendices
GAUDIEMPRE	20/6/18		In consequence of the reduction of teams of 18/- + 4.5 how ammunition G.S. wagons 36 men & 72 animals became surplus to establishment. 24 men + 51 animals were sent to the Base, & the remaining 12 men + 25 animals absorbed into the strength of the 40th Divl Arty	1125/28
BARLY	24/6/18		S.A.A. Section. The following Officers proceeded to the Base in connection with the reforming of the S.A.A. Section. Lt A.H.Orrell No 1 Section Lt J.H.Pelham No 2 Section 2/Lt D.S.Kempton No 1 Section 18/- 9886 rds 4.5 how 2780 rds AMMUNITION Ammunition as under was delivered by lochons to Batteries during the month	
BARLY	24/6/18		DIVL.T.M.BATTERIES Lt J.E. Benningfield reported here 24/6/18 from D/178 Bde for the purpose of reforming the 40th Divl Trench Mortar Batteries. The present strength is 4 Officers 76 other ranks.	

Army Form C. 2118.

WAR DIARY
or
INTELLIGENCE SUMMARY.
(Erase heading not required.)

Instructions regarding War Diaries and Intelligence Summaries are contained in F. S. Regs., Part II. and the Staff Manual respectively. Title pages will be prepared in manuscript.

Place	Date	Hour	Summary of Events and Information	Remarks and references to Appendices
			Training is being proceeded with	
			CASUALTIES	
			NIL	
			R.R. [signature]	
			LT. COLONEL, R.F.A.	
			COMDG. 40TH DIVL. AMM. COLUMN.	

Confidential

40th Divl Amn Col R.F.A

WAR DIARY
or
INTELLIGENCE SUMMARY.

Army Form C. 2118.

Rebated 31.2 / 40000

VOL 26

Place	Date	Hour	Summary of Events and Information	Remarks and references to Appendices
FOSSEUX			**RELIEFS**	
	26.7.18		HQ 40th Divl Arty relieved the 3rd Canadian Artillery & the 3 sections came under the orders of the 40th DRA 40th Div	Order No 1444
			The ARP at R.26.b.7.8 was taken over from the 3rd Canadian D.A & Lt Tloyd (NC) was placed in charge.	
			In consequence of the withdrawal from the line of the 232nd Army Brigade, the 175th Bde R.F.A. & No.1 Section 40th D.A.C. came under orders of the 40th Divl Arty	Order No 1447
	31.7.18		Headquarters 40th DAC moved from FOSSEUX to Q.13.c.9.8	
			S.A.A. Section	
		16.15	The reforming of the S.A.A. Section having been completed the Section joined the Division ahead	
			CASUALTIES NIL	

R.R.Atman
LT. COLONEL, R.F.A.

WAR DIARY
INTELLIGENCE SUMMARY

HQ Park Amm Col RFA

AUGUST 1918

Army Form C. 2118.

Place	Date	Hour	Summary of Events and Information	Remarks and references to Appendices
GOUY	1/8	—	MOVES	
			Convened in the central wood S. of farmhouse A27 Montrecourt road	
			To General Note R28c 7.4	
			TO MILLS – 8	
			AMMUNITION	
			The supply of ammunition was carried on as usual	
			14th – Sent 100 18/pdr cart. to [illegible] by 8.00am	
			on A27 for convoy to [illegible]	
			In addition to delivery ammunition on convoys	
			to 186 DAC & 119 AS, HQ Bn 1 BS. 930 [illegible]	
			OTHERS	
			[illegible]	
			HOPE Lieut [illegible] joined left strength unaffected from the	
			[illegible] and Kings LR London	
			CASUALTIES	
			The unmentioned were accurately injured 27.8.18	
			80138 Lft W.J Haig B.A.C.	
			184314 Dr Batchelor L.A.L. HQ Staff	
			RWS Ruddin	
			R R Oliver	

LT. COLONEL, R.F.A.
COMDG. 40TH DIV. AMM. COLUMN

Confidential

Sht I

Army Form C. 2118.

H.Q.ʳᵈ D.A.C.R.F.A.   WAR DIARY   SEPTEMBER 1918
or
INTELLIGENCE SUMMARY. Ref sheets 51ᴮ. 57ᴰ. 1/40,000

(Erase heading not required.)

Vol 28

Place	Date	Hour	Summary of Events and Information	Remarks and references to Appendices
Barlantot	1/9/18		In conformity with the development of operations the D.A.C. moves as under:-	
	3/9/18		To T.16.c.3.1.	
	19/9/18		To C.7.d.6.2.	
	21/9/18		To D.20.d.9.1.	
	25/9/18		To E.27.a.5.4.	
	30/9/18		To E.24.c.6.5.	

During this period the D.A.C. delivered ammunition to batteries, salvaged ammunition left in vacated gun positions, & also German gun shells for use with captured 77 m/m guns.
The following are the amounts:-
Ammunition delivered to Batteries 25,652 18pdr + 11,100 now 4.5 how.
Salvaged ammunition 9563 18pdr. 898 A.S. 1634 Bx 200 gas.
German 77 m/m gas shells 4500 rds.
Various A.R.Ps were staffed by the D.A.C. as the situation necessitated

Army Form C. 2118.

WAR DIARY
or
INTELLIGENCE SUMMARY
(Erase heading not required.)

Place	Date	Hour	Summary of Events and Information	Remarks and references to Appendices
			CASUALTIES Officers NIL Other ranks No 68644 Sgt. G.W. Marsden M.M. No.1 Section wounded by hostile shell fire 24/9/18 No 42089 Gr. F. Timmins No.1 Section wounded by hostile shell fire 25/9/18 HONOURS & AWARDS The XVII Corps Commander awarded the Military Medal to the undermentioned No 47291 L/Bdr Marsland J. No. 2 Section No 35749 Gnr. Sug. T.H.M. No. 2 Section K.F.Clement LT. COLONEL, COMDG. 40TH DIVL. AMM. COLUMN.	

Sheet I

Army Form C. 2118.

HQ D.A.C. R.F.A. WAR DIARY OCTOBER 1918

INTELLIGENCE SUMMARY. Refsheets 57B 57C 36A 36 37 } 1/40,000

(Erase heading not required.)

Instructions regarding War Diaries and Intelligence Summaries are contained in F. S. Regs., Part II. and the Staff Manual respectively. Title pages will be prepared in manuscript.

Place	Date	Hour	Summary of Events and Information	Remarks and references to Appendices
			MOVEMENTS	
	10/10/18		The D.A.C. moved in conformity with the tactical situation	
	10/10/18		To A 26 a 9.4	
			To B 11 c 3.1	
	13/10/18		The 40th Div'l. Arty. was relieved by the 61st Div'l. Arty. & Hd S. were	
	15/10/18		To A 26 a 9.4	
			Entraining orders having been received the D.a.c moved to I.5 a 0.2 on the 16/10/18 & entrained as follows, for the 2nd Army Area, to join the 40th Div.	
	16/10/18		H.Q. Staff Entrained at FREMICOURT	
			Hy. Section Entrained at BAPAUME	
			between at STEENBECQUE detrained at THIENNES	
	19/10/18		Hd Qrs proceeded to D 15 c 6.6 & from thence to	
	21/10/18		To A 11 c 9.0	
	22/10/18		To B 20 c 9.8	
	23/10/18		To E 26 a 9.6	
	26/10/18		The 151st Brigade R.F.A. relieved one Brigade of the 31st Div'l. Arty. & Hd 2 Section moved to A 26 & 6.5	

Army Form C. 2118.

Sheet II

40th D.A.C. RFA WAR DIARY
or
~~INTELLIGENCE~~ SUMMARY.

(Erase heading not required.)

Instructions regarding War Diaries and Intelligence Summaries are contained in F. S. Regs., Part II. and the Staff Manual respectively. Title pages will be prepared in manuscript.

Place	Date	Hour	Summary of Events and Information	Remarks and references to Appendices
	25/10/18		H.Q. Staff moved to 915 6 9 9 7	
	20/10/18		S.A.A. Section	
			S.A.A. Section came under the 40th Divl. Arty. for administration 20/10/18	
			INSPECTION	
			The G.O.C. 40th Divl. inspected the S.A.A. 24/10/18	
	24/10/18		A.R.P.	
			On arrival in XV Corps area two. A.R.Ps. were taken over & staffed.	
			CASUALTIES	
			NIL	

R.R. ~~Stewart~~
LT. COLONEL, R.F.A.
OC/CG. 40TH DIVL. AMM. COLUMN.

Confidential

HOR DAC R.F.A.

WAR DIARY
or
INTELLIGENCE SUMMARY.
(Erase heading not required.)

November 1918

Army Form C. 2118.

Ref sheets 37 & 36 'Serouve'

Vol 30

Instructions regarding War Diaries and Intelligence Summaries are contained in F. S. Regs., Part II. and the Staff Manual respectively. Title pages will be prepared in manuscript.

Place	Date	Hour	Summary of Events and Information	Remarks and references to Appendices
LANNOY	9/11/18		**MOVEMENTS**	
			No. 1 Section moved to A 26 b. 6. 5	
	9/11/18		Headquarters to SOS, moved to A 26 b. 2. 6.	
	15/11/18		The HQ & No S.A.A. Sections moved to vicinity of E 26 d. & billeted as under	HQ DA order Bn 175
			Headquarters E 26 d. 5.6	
			No 1 Section E 26 d. 7.9	
			No 2 Section N 9 c 3.3	
			ARMISTICE	
	11/11/18		T.R. Armistice came into operation at 11.00 hours	
			CASUALTIES	
			NIL	

R.P. Stewart
LT. COLONEL, R.F.A.
COMDG. 40TH DIVL. AMM. COLUMN.

Confidential

Army Form C. 2118.

4th DACTRFA

WAR DIARY
or
INTELLIGENCE SUMMARY.

December 1918

Ref sheet 36 1/40000

(Erase heading not required.)

Instructions regarding War Diaries and Intelligence Summaries are contained in F. S. Regs., Part II. and the Staff Manual respectively. Title pages will be prepared in manuscript.

Place	Date	Hour	Summary of Events and Information	Remarks and references to Appendices
WIMEREUX			**MOVEMENTS** The SAA Section moved to Huc 6.3 sh 7b	Vol 31
			CASUALTIES Nil	
			TRAINING Training has been proceeded with but has to be greatly curtailed by the number of men away on detachment.	

J.W. Whittaker Lt Col
Commanding 4th Div. Amm. Col. R.F.A.

40th D.A.C. R.F.A. January 1919

Army Form C. 2118.

WAR DIARY
or
INTELLIGENCE SUMMARY.
(Erase heading not required.)

Instructions regarding War Diaries and Intelligence Summaries are contained in F. S. Regs., Part II. and the Staff Manual respectively. Title pages will be prepared in manuscript.

Vol 32

Place	Date	Hour	Summary of Events and Information	Remarks and references to Appendices
Wimbledon			NIL	

CAPT. R.F.A.
ADJUTANT, 40th DIV/ AMMN. COL. R.F.A.

Army Form C. 2118.

WAR DIARY
or
INTELLIGENCE SUMMARY.
(Erase heading not required.)

40 D Amm Col

Instructions regarding War Diaries and Intelligence Summaries are contained in F. S. Regs., Part II. and the Staff Manual respectively. Title pages will be prepared in manuscript.

Place	Date	Hour	Summary of Events and Information	Remarks and references to Appendices
			Nil	

T. Thos
CAPT. R.F.A.
ADJUTANT 40TH DIV AMMN. COL. B.E.F.

Army Form C. 2118.

WAR DIARY
or
INTELLIGENCE SUMMARY.
(Erase heading not required.)

Instructions regarding War Diaries and Intelligence Summaries are contained in F. S. Regs., Part II. and the Staff Manual respectively. Title pages will be prepared in manuscript.

Place	Date	Hour	Summary of Events and Information	Remarks and references to Appendices

40th Divisional Artillery.

WAR DIARY

40th DIVISIONAL AMMUNITION COLUMN R.F.A.

APRIL 1 9 1 8

Confidential

40th D.A.C. R.F.A. Rifleshot 51c
{36D, 36D} 4,000
from 11
Hazebrouck 5 of 1/100,000

Army Form C. 2118.

WAR DIARY
or
INTELLIGENCE SUMMARY.
(Erase heading not required.)

Vol 23

Place	Date	Hour	Summary of Events and Information	Remarks and references to Appendices
GOUY EN ARTOIS			H.Q. Staff & Hd. Section moved to GOUY EN ARTOIS	
			DAC Coy SAA Section moved to REBREUVIETTE	
			No 2 Section came under orders of 2nd Canadian DAC moved to GOUY EN ARTOIS	
			No 1 Section came under orders of 3rd Canadian DAC Headquarters Staff	
			5 Section moved to SAULTY	
			Headquarters Left the Section moved to BETHLEHEM BOIS	
			On relinquishment of the Horse Lines R.Hy. taking over command of Horse Dump & 12 ART. at BLAIREVILLE and the Ammunition Dump & 1 SHRAPNEL CORNER came under the orders of the DAC they were disposed as follows	
			BLAIREVILLE DUMP	
			1 Officer	
			31 Rccuy men attached	
			12 Batteries Exp X/D/7, H D	
			SHRAPNEL CORNER	
			1 NCO +	

Army Form C. 2118.

WAR DIARY
or
INTELLIGENCE SUMMARY.
(Erase heading not required.)

Instructions regarding War Diaries and Intelligence Summaries are contained in F. S. Regs., Part II. and the Staff Manual respectively. Title pages will be prepared in manuscript.

Place	Date	Hour	Summary of Events and Information	Remarks and references to Appendices

Army Form C. 2118.

WAR DIARY
or
INTELLIGENCE SUMMARY.
(Erase heading not required.)

Instructions regarding War Diaries and Intelligence Summaries are contained in F. S. Regs., Part II. and the Staff Manual respectively. Title pages will be prepared in manuscript.

Place	Date	Hour	Summary of Events and Information	Remarks and references to Appendices
			There was did not enter as north the delivery of ammunition to the station arriving at a new camp, dumps were made towards the road. During the period over 2,300,000 rds of ammunition were issued.	
Casualties				
			The following casualties occurred:—	
			Killed 1 native driver	
			Wounded Lt. T. Thorpe (of duty) + two natives	
			INCC 2 Rebel Gunners + two natives.	

R. R. Stewart
LT. COLONEL, R.F.A.
COMDG. 46th BDE. ARMY COLUMN.

www.ingramcontent.com/pod-product-compliance
Lightning Source LLC
Chambersburg PA
CBHW081555160426
43191CB00011B/1934